A Parent's Guide
to Understanding and
Motivating Children

Amy Lew, Ph.D.
and
Betty Lou Bettner, Ph.D.

Connexions Press

Acknowledgment

The authors are indebted to Alfred Adler and Rudolf Dreikurs for developing the concepts that provide the inspiration for this work.

ISBN 0-9624841-8-0

Connexions Press   &   Connexions Press
10 Langley Road, Ste. 200   1 Old State Road
Newton Centre, MA 02459   Media, PA 19063
tel.: 617-332-3220   tel.: 610-566-1004
fax: 617-332-7863   fax: 610-566-1004
e-mail: connexpr@thecia.net   e-mail: blbettner@aol.com

CONTENTS

What Can Parents Do to Protect Children?..............................1
  A dangerous world for children—and parents..........................1
  Giving children what they need..2
Four Vital Protections: The Crucial Cs....................................4
  The enduring need to be connected..4
  The need to develop competence and feel capable......................8
  The essential need for significance; the belief that one counts........11
  The lifelong need for courage...14
  Essential skills and abilities..17
Understanding Behaviors as Ways of Seeking to Fulfill Needs......22
  The goals of misbehavior...23
  Why is the goal important?...26
  How does the child develop mistaken goals?............................28
  Attention...28
  Power..33
  Revenge...37
  Avoidance..42
Developing Self-Esteem through Encouragement.....................45
  Encouragement versus evaluative praise.................................46
Helping Children to Feel the Crucial Cs................................48
  Helping the child feel connected..48
  Helping the child feel capable...50
  Helping the child feel he or she counts...................................51
  Helping the child develop courage..53
Logical Discipline...54
  Consequences versus punishment...55
  On the subject of hitting...57
Preparing Children to Live in a Democracy...........................61
Family Meeting Guidelines..64
How Can Parents Work with Schools?..................................68
Appendices...70
  The Crucial Cs and Dreikurs'
    Short-Range Goals of Misbehavior...................................70
  The Crucial Cs Chart...72
  Recommended reading..73
  About the authors...75
  Other books by Amy Lew and Betty Lou Bettner.....................76
  Ordering Information...78

What Can Parents Do to Protect Children?

A dangerous world for children—and parents

It's a jungle out there for kids—we all know that. It's a jungle out there for parents, too, but that reality gets less attention. The pressures and conflicts of life today combine to make fulfilling our responsibilities as parents extremely difficult, just as they combine to make growing up into a responsible adult extremely difficult for a child.

Some people argue that nothing has changed, that the central tasks of growing up and parenting have always been the most difficult tasks of life. Perhaps so, but our time is plagued with dire threats of loss, catastrophic threats to economic, social, and spiritual survival. Job loss, drugs, AIDS, homelessness, the weakening of value systems, and other forces imperil people's lives and pull family members and entire families under.

The family itself may also feel like a jungle—for both parents and children—as the problems of the environment move into the home and begin to defeat caring, cooperation, and good will. Financial and emotional scarcity often leads family members to compete instead of cooperate, demand instead of negotiate, take instead of give and take. When these forces take hold, family life begins to seem as unstable as a house of cards, with each added stress threatening to bring down the whole structure.

Not surprisingly then, there is a lot of concern about the future. Parents worry about the high incidence of teenage drug and alcohol abuse, teen gangs and violence, and the general alienation of our youth. They also worry about the growing number of divorces and teen parents and the "me first" attitude of many of our young people.

These grim trends cause all of us serious concern. But as marriage and family therapists who are actively involved in parent and teacher education, and as parents ourselves, we are optimistic. We believe that parents can still manage to be good parents and have personally fulfilling lives, and that children can still accomplish their major developmental tasks and become productive, happy adults in satisfying relationships. This book is about how parents can carry out this process successfully.

The parenting approach we advocate does not tell parents to lay down the law, make stricter rules, and demand obedience. As any parent of teenagers knows, it's a lot easier to *make* the rules than to *enforce* them, so parents are often discouraged by this advice. When they try to make their children behave, the kids escalate their defiance or withdraw and hide what they are doing. Whatever positive relationship there may have been is eroded by the parents' becoming distrustful law enforcers, and whatever respect the children may have had for the parents is eroded by the parents' laying down laws they can't enforce. If law enforcement isn't the answer, then what do children need and what can parents do?

Giving children what they need

Several years ago some research was undertaken to discover why some children become successful and others do not. The findings are very clear regarding those differences: children who succeed have close relationships to others, feel valued in their communities, and have a sense of control over some aspects of their lives; children who are in trouble feel isolated, useless to society, and powerless.

The kids in trouble are missing four necessities that each child must have in order to successfully meet life's challenges. These necessities are not rules, not something children have to master and consciously remember. They are beliefs that parents can foster in their children that will serve as unconscious behavioral guides. These beliefs are the internal certainty of—

• Being **connected** to others, a part of family and community,
• Having the **capability** to take care of oneself,
• Being valued by others, the knowledge that one **counts**
  and makes a difference, and
• Having **courage**.

We call these four vital protections—**connection, capability, counting,** and **courage**—the **Crucial Cs** because they are the foundation for raising kids who can meet the challenges of these difficult times and become—

• Responsible	• Resilient
• Productive	• Resourceful
• Cooperative	• Contributing
• Self-reliant	• Happy

We will look first at how these vital attributes help to protect children in childhood and enable them to become adults capable of contributing to family and society. We will look at what parents can do to impart this internal protection to their children and foster the growth of their capacities to lead rewarding adult lives. We will also give parents a guide for understanding why children behave as they do.

The parenting approach we recommend not only helps children meet developmental goals; it helps parents to lead lives of achievement and fulfillment, as well. What we present here is a blueprint for parenting and conducting family life that is beneficial to both.

Four Vital Protections: The Crucial Cs

The enduring need to be connected

Human beings are social animals. Since we have no shell, no claws, no fangs, and no wings and since we are not stronger or faster than our enemies, we have had to band together for survival. We need to experience this connection for both physical and psychological security. Our survival depends on our ability to connect with others. This theme of dependence on connection with others takes different forms at different stages of life, but it runs throughout our lives.

Developmentally, the most important task is to move from being totally dependent on others to being interdependent with others. This is not only for our own survival but to ensure the survival of the species. Therefore, necessity dictates that as soon as possible members of the social group make contributions to the group as well as take benefits from it. The nature of our connection then shifts from being dependent on others to becoming someone upon whom others can depend.

Infancy. The human infant's first need is to be connected, and if this first need is not met, the child will die. We cannot lift our heads at birth, much less crawl about in search of food. And our dependence on being connected to another is by no means limited to mealtimes. We are dependent on others for protection, shelter, and training in the skills we will need to take care of ourselves. This process of moving from dependence to independence takes a relatively long time.

Beyond the basic physical needs, the baby has emotional needs as well, and these, too, are met only in relationships. Bonding with the caregiver is the first way in which these needs are met. Nature serves the infant especially well here because bonding is also the caregiver's earliest emotional reward for performing the demanding task of providing for the newborn.

When an infant's needs to be held, caressed, and talked to are not met, the infant's capacity to relate to others will not develop. In time the child may withdraw into a state of remoteness in which he or she may not be *able* to connect with others. When all of these needs are met from the beginning, however, the baby will thrive and develop to full potential.

The job of the primary caregiver through this first connection is to ensure the survival of the infant while it is totally depen-dent and to foster the opportunities for the child to gain the capacity for greater independence and later interdependence.

Childhood. As infants grow they begin to develop their capabilities and move from total dependence towards a greater capacity for independence. Children must, however, develop new ways to connect to others so that they can take their place in society. Childhood is the time to actively experiment with different ways of relating and to try out various forms and degrees of both independence and interdependence. Through this process of trial and error, the child arrives at a set of beliefs about the world and what is possible, a strategy for living, and a set of behaviors to carry out the strategy.

Children who develop positive feelings of connection with their families have the confidence they need to reach out to others, make friends, and cooperate. When they are grown, they are more likely to develop mutually supportive, intimate relationships.

Children who are unsure of their ability to connect with others may feel insecure, isolated, and scared. They will do whatever they think they have to do to find a place. This may mean being the "perfect" child, the "bad" child, the clown, the scapegoat, or any number of other roles. They may seek attention to prove they have a place. The main point is that each of us develops an idea about what we must do in order to connect to those we depend upon.

Even in a family where the child is neglected or abused, the child must find someone with whom to connect in order to survive and to achieve psychological security. A child in a dysfunctional family does not realize that his or her family is different from others. Some children will connect with an abuser who appears to have the power; others will align themselves with a parent who doesn't protect them but shows concern.

Adolescence. As children enter adolescence and their teen years, we can clearly see the effects of their beliefs about belonging and connection. Young people who are confident about their place in the group are able to participate and cooperate. They can be leaders or followers depending on the needs of the situation. These teens are able to decide when to go along with the crowd and when to say no because they are not afraid that they will be rejected or isolated. Youth who do not feel secure about their ability to connect are more susceptible to peer pressure. They believe that they must go along with the crowd or be ostracized.

Does the child CONNECT in a constructive way?

The child who does not connect in a constructive way—

The child who connects in a constructive way—

- Feels **insecure**
- Feels isolated
- Is more susceptible to peer pressure
- Seeks **attention**
- May conclude that connecting in a negative way is better than not connecting at all

- Feels **secure**
- Can reach out
- Can make friends

- Can **cooperate**

If the child believes that he or she can connect in a positive way, the child does connect constructively.

Children who connect in a constructive way can say with conviction, "I believe that I belong."

This need for connection was underscored by the findings of the National Longitudinal Study on Adolescent Health which were presented in a paper entitled "Protecting Adolescents from Harm" published in the *Journal of the American Medical Association* (vol. 278, no.10, September 10, 1997, pp. 823 ff.). Based on interviews with over 12,000 adolescents in grades 7 through 12, the study identified risk and protective factors in the areas of emotional health, violence, substance use (alcohol, cigarettes, marijuana), and sexuality. The researchers looked at the family, the school, and the individual and found that parent-family connectedness and the perceived connectedness of school with young people were protective against every risk studied with the exception of pregnancy. (Concerning pregnancy, the study found that parental disapproval of early sexual activity was associated with delay of intercourse.)

The need to develop competence and feel capable

If people are to move along the road from dependence to interdependence, they must also develop the ability to be independent. When we refer to "independence" in human beings, we mean some degree of self-sufficiency in performing certain tasks. The developing child's achievements in the direction of independence and the increasing capacity to take care of oneself are the foundation of the belief in oneself as competent and capable.

Infancy. Infants who begin life only able to cry, squirm, and suck gradually learn to hold up their heads, roll over, stand, and walk. No one has to force them to try; they do it for the pure joy of it. We only have to watch a young child learning to walk to realize that this drive to develop toward independence is innate. Nobody else could reward us enough to get us to fall down as often as we do while learning to walk; and yet, as children, we try over and over and each step brings with it the reward of accomplishment usually evidenced by an enormous grin!

Childhood. As children grow they must be given opportunities to develop their competence through real jobs

8

and activities. Parents who are often stressed and in a hurry may find it easier to do things themselves, but this mistake may have dire consequences. Children may interpret parents' failure to assign them meaningful work as a vote of no confidence in their ability to do things themselves. They also may compare themselves to adults and older siblings who seem to be able to do everything and decide that since they are not as capable as others, they shouldn't even bother to try. If they decide that others are trying to keep them dependent, they may feel resentful or inadequate. Worse, they may comfortably settle into the role of pampered child with no responsibilities.

These children may become overly dependent on others or may allow others to treat them disrespectfully because they are afraid to be on their own. They may interpret others' behavior as controlling whether it is or not. They may become so confused that they believe that control is a sign of competence and independence. Moreover, they may become so impressed with the idea of control that they'll try to show their own power by bossing others or proving that others can't tell them what to do. They may respond to even an ordinary request as if it were an unreasonable demand.

Adolescence. Young people who develop their competence in a supportive atmosphere will develop self-control and become self-reliant. They will be able and willing to assume responsibility and enter into respectful and equal relationships. In contrast, teens who are unsure of their competence may try to prove it by taking unnecessary risks. They may resist any attempt to guide them, trying instead to show the world that they can do whatever they want and can handle whatever comes their way. Some discouraged teens take another tack and try to get others to excuse them from responsibility and give them special

9

consideration, e.g., getting them up in the morning, picking up after them, reminding them to do their homework, repeatedly delivering forgotten lunches.

Does the child believe himself or herself to be CAPABLE?

The child who does not believe in his or her capability—

The child who believes in his or her capability—

- Feels **inadequate**
- Tries to control others and/or becomes defiant ("You can't make me!")
- May become dependent

- Seeks **power**

- Feels **competent**
- Has self-control and self-discipline

- Assumes responsibility
- Is **self-reliant**

If the child believes in his or her competence, the child behaves capably.

Children who believe they are capable can say with conviction, "I believe that I can do it."

Children will *always* come up with some way to feel capable and the form it takes will be based on the choices they made earlier in life about how to connect. Sometimes people achieve only the capability of getting others to take care of them. Others may become capable by being "enablers," who always care for others first. Becoming capable can take many forms, some clearly more satisfactory than others.

The essential need for significance; the belief that one counts

The third necessity is to feel significant, to count. All of us want to feel that we make a difference, that our existence matters. We want to believe that we will be missed if we don't show up.

Infancy. Human beings begin their lives totally self-centered. Their main occupation is to get their needs met. Infants are unable to differentiate themselves from others: they see others only in relation to themselves. If adults care for them and respond to their needs, they develop a feeling of security. They learn that they can count on others and that their wellbeing is important to their caregivers. In the early years, babies' experience of counting is pretty one-sided. They do, however, begin to make conclusions about what caring for others entails. If they are treated with consideration and respect, they will find it easier to bond with others. If they are ignored or mistreated, they may be so involved with getting their needs met that they may not be able to move beyond their own self-centered world.

Childhood. As children grow and develop their capabilities, they also try to participate in family and group life. If their attempts to take part and help out are appreciated and encouraged, they will derive their feeling of significance through membership and contribution. Their self-esteem will develop because they feel valued by others and they know that they can make a difference.

When children don't believe that they can make meaningful contributions, they may come to believe that they are insignificant. The need to feel significant is so strong that children, discouraged by the belief that they can't make a difference by constructive means, will find other ways to make their mark. They may give up trying to participate in helpful ways and try to prove that they count by intimidating others or by inflating their own importance by acting superior. Misbehaviors such as provoking others and seeking revenge are all ways of showing that they do count for something.

Adolescence. Teenagers who believe that they can make a difference in their families and in the world are eager to get involved. These young adults often become active in school and community service. They are conscious of how their behavior affects others and the world around them. They are less likely to break laws or to try to avoid responsibility because they realize that their behavior has consequences. They also see the value of voting, of developing their skills, and of participating in their community because they know they can make a difference.

Remember, people who don't believe that they can count through constructive means try to prove that they count through negative means. We're well aware of the dangers of that belief in adolescence. Teenage girls may become sexually active as a way of getting someone to care about them. Some even choose to have a baby in order to feel that someone needs them. Some teenage boys may try to get girls pregnant in order to feel that they have done something important. Vandalism and other disruptive behavior can also be ways to have an impact on those around you.

Even teens who don't actively try to prove that they count through destructive behavior are at risk. They may refuse to cooperate or to work towards any meaningful goals because they believe that nothing they do really matters. If they throw their trash out the window, who cares? It's only a little trash. Why should they care about the environment? Nobody cares anything about them. If they don't do their chores, who cares? Someone else can do them. What difference does it make if they vote? It's only one vote. Nothing ever changes anyway.

Does the child believe that he or she COUNTS in a constructive way?

The child who believes that he or she does not count in a constructive way—

The child who believes that he or she counts in a constructive way—

- Feels **insignificant** and **hurt**
- May try to hurt back

- May seek **revenge**

- May conclude that making a negative impact is better than making no impact

- Feels **valuable**
- Believes he or she can make a difference in a constructive way
- Can **contribute** constructively

If the child believes that he or she counts in a positive way, the child behaves constructively.

Children who believe that they count in constructive ways can say with conviction, "I believe that I matter and I can make a difference."

Children will always come up with some ways to feel that they count. Here again, the form it takes will be based on the choices they made earlier in life about what they must do to connect and what they are capable of. If we want our children to make constructive choices, to take their place in society, and to become good citizens, they must believe that their opinions and actions matter.

The lifelong need for courage

Human development from infancy to adulthood, and, indeed, to the end of life, is a complex and risky undertaking, a journey filled with trial and error and trial again until the person finds a way that works. It is a journey that takes a great amount of courage.

Courage, then, is the fourth of the "Crucial Cs." How important is it to leading a constructive life? It is so important that Rudolf Dreikurs, renowned psychiatrist and parent educator, said that if we could give children only one quality to get them through life, courage would be the most necessary.

Infancy and childhood. The early signs of courage appear after every unsuccessful developmental effort the infant makes. Nothing the infant undertakes is successful on the first try except by accident, and mastery requires many, many trials.

Infants and children must possess a great amount of courage in order to keep trying to achieve what they need and want to do. This fact becomes obvious when we recall their faces and voices as they encounter major failure in their efforts (a scraped knee, a bumped head, or a buckling leg when learning to walk; the inability to make themselves understood when learning to talk; the physical and emotional hurt of falling off a bike when learning to ride).

Another way we can get some idea of the life-sustaining role courage plays in human development is to recall some of our own emotions upon confronting very difficult tasks in childhood—going to school for the first time, taking the bus or subway alone, getting lost and needing help, learning to swim. Remember the fear or perhaps terror you felt one of those times when you wanted to accomplish something very much. Did you go forward in spite of the fear? Did you give up or avoid the situation?

Hurt, anger, frustration, disappointment, and fear are all emotions human beings experience very early in life. In the course of learning, infants and children have more experiences of failure than of success. It's a wonder that they keep trying, and that wonder is called courage. For babies and children to develop as fully as possible, they must have the courage to press on in the face of failure and fear. Courage is not the absence of fear; courage is the willingness to go forward and do what needs to be done in spite of the fear.

Children without courage focus on what they can't do. They often give up and try to avoid reminders of their feelings of fear and failure by getting others to give up on them, too. Infants and children with courage develop resiliency. They feel hopeful, are willing to take reasonable risks and try new things, and try them again after failure.

Adolescence. Adolescence is a time of great confusion and uncertainty. One foot is still in childhood, the other tentatively seeking a toehold in adulthood only to become off-balance and to land back in childhood. One step forward and two steps back, two steps forward and two steps back, then eventually two steps forward and one step back. Such is the nature of teenage progress.

The teenager probably is struggling with the time-honored problems of sexuality, the competing demands of family membership and peer-group membership, the dependence-versus-independence dilemma in its many forms, and so on. The teenager in today's society may also be struggling with the newer problems posed by the prevalence of violence, teen suicide, drugs, alcohol, dress standards, and other harsh realities.

The fear of AIDS besets some young people as they think about or engage in sexual exploration—and even worse, some don't worry about it at all. Prevalent ideas about how bodies should look may lead some to eating disorders and others to steroid usage.

The amount of courage teens need to deal with the issues that are appropriate to their age is enormous. The amount of courage required of teens who face some of the life-threatening challenges we've named here is of heroic proportions.

Adolescents without courage don't speak in class for fear of being wrong—or, where there is a culture of disdain for school among the students, some don't speak for fear of being right. Teens who lack courage probably will not be able to resist pressure to take drugs or drink alcohol or shoplift or play with guns. Adolescents with courage have the strength they need to face life's challenges and difficulties and go against the crowd when the situation requires it. Adolescents with courage can say no to unwanted sexual advances. They can refuse to travel with the crowd when the driver has been drinking

Does the child have COURAGE?

The child who does not have courage—	The child who has courage—
• Cannot overcome fear	• Overcomes fear
• Feels **inferior, defeated, hopeless,** and **discouraged**	• Feels **equal, confident,** and **hopeful**
• May give up, use **avoidance**	• Faces challenges, is **resilient**
• May be afraid to go against the crowd	• Can stand alone if necessary

If the child has courage, he or she can carry out the learning and sustain the effort that life requires.

Children with courage can say with conviction, "I believe that I can handle what comes."

Essential skills and abilities

In order for the Crucial Cs to be fulfilled constructively, a person must also develop four important sets of skills.

1. COMMUNICATION skills. These skills include being able to talk, to express ourselves, and to listen to others. Communication is required in all of our life tasks—in making and keeping friends, on the job, and in intimate relationships. We have to be able to listen, cooperate, negotiate, share, empathize.

The number one reason people lose their jobs, other than major cutbacks, is due to poor interpersonal skills—they don't know how to get along with others. The major reason friendships break up is poor communication. When people get divorced, what do they usually give as the reason? "We couldn't communicate." What is the biggest complaint that we hear between adults and children? "You don't understand me."

We need to be able to communicate, to be able to **connect**.

Without communication skills, people lose jobs and can't maintain relationships.

2. **SELF-DISCIPLINE**. Self-control enables children to master their emotions and behavior in order to achieve positive goals for themselves and for the community. Self-discipline enables the person to work for something in the present so that he or she can achieve something in the future. It also means holding off getting or doing what you want right now because it might interfere with achieving your long-term goals—such as not getting that expensive pair of sneakers because you're saving for college or a special trip. Self-discipline is an antidote to wanting instant gratification.

Children with self-discipline are in control of themselves. They can control feelings like anger and aggression so that they don't use them self-destructively or to hurt others. They can put their feelings to work to motivate themselves and help change what needs to be changed. Self-disciplined children develop inner strength and are able to resist negative pressures and temptations. They can succeed at school and get and keep jobs.

We need self-discipline to become **capable**.

Without this characteristic people feel out of control, vulnerable, at the mercy of luck and fate.

3. **ASSUMING RESPONSIBILITY**. This includes the ability and willingness to see what needs to be done and to do it, setting goals and following through. Children must learn the difference between rights and privileges, and the responsibility that goes with each.

Kids must also learn to take responsibility for their actions. They should not be able to excuse their behavior by blaming others—"It was her idea!" "He made me do it!" "They told me I should!" "I was only following orders!"—or by depending on others to think for them or protect them from dangers—"You should have told me before!" "I thought he knew how to drive!" "I thought Jana had asked her mother to pick us up!"

When children do well in school, they should know it is because they did the work and when they do poorly, they should be able to analyze their mistakes. They also need to learn from their experiences, fix what they can, and decide what they will do differently in the future. Leadership and high productivity depend on assuming responsibility.

We need to believe that we **count** and make a difference if we are going to be willing to assume responsibility.

Without this ability, people tend to feel overburdened and focus on life's being unfair.

4. The ability to use **GOOD JUDGMENT** and **MAKE WISE DECISIONS**. This set of skills requires being open to facts and others' ideas and being able to look at options, weigh various possibilities, and make reasonable choices.

We are bombarded every day with endless choices—on grocery shelves, in shopping malls, and on television. The workplace also reflects this trend. As more and more jobs are automated, there is less need for people who are good at following orders or rote repetition. Employers want people who are able to figure things out and to think for themselves. More important, as citizens of a democracy, we are called upon to exercise judgment and make decisions about competing ideas. We must be able to decide who is trustworthy, how to vote, and what to believe. To live in today's world, one must be able to think through problems and make responsible choices. Our behavioral responses determine how we will be in relation to others—our friends, family, and the larger society—essentially, how we want and will try to live our lives.

Good judgment is essential if children are to be able to decide if something is safe or dangerous, fair or unfair, appropriate or inappropriate, moral or immoral, ethical or unethical. Children need good judgment to help decide when to go along with the group and when to stand up for what they know is right. They need to be able to decide when they should lead, when they should follow, and when they should go it alone.

Today's society holds many dangers for our children. Newspapers are full of stories about kids faced with abuse, drugs, alcohol, sexual activity, and other forms of violence. We can no longer depend on other adults to watch out for our children. We can't simply teach kids to always respect their elders and do what any grown-up says. We must teach them to evaluate situations, consider consequences, and decide for themselves.

We need good judgment if we are going to use our **courage** wisely. We must be able to decide when to persevere, when to shift direction, when to fight for something, and when to withdraw.

Without good judgment, kids are more vulnerable to peer pressure, joining cults and gangs, and being taken advantage of by unscrupulous adults.

The development of these four sets of skills and qualities, which are critical to a person's life, should not be left to chance. They need to be cultivated and nurtured. Although nothing we can do guarantees that our children will turn out exactly the way we want them to, we *can* increase the likelihood of producing capable, well adjusted young people *if* we put thought and effort into our parenting techniques.

The first thing we need to do is to evaluate our current approach to see if it promotes the development of the qualities that we have seen to be critical. We can accomplish this evaluation by answering the following questions about our current parenting techniques.

1. Are they stopping misbehavior?

2. Are they developing the qualities I want to foster in my child?

3. What kind of opinion does my child seem to be forming of himself or herself and others?

4. Does my child act as a contributing member of society, or as if the world is here to serve him or her?

If one or more of the answers to these questions is or are unsatisfactory, we must come up with a new approach.

Understanding Behaviors
as Ways of Seeking to Fulfill Needs

All human beings strive to fulfill their needs to be connected to others, to be capable of a degree of independence, to count as a member of the family and the community, and to find the courage to meet life's demands and seize its opportunities. As infants and children, we try out various behaviors to get these needs met. We learn that some behaviors get responses and some don't, and that some behaviors get better responses than others.

When constructive behaviors bring the desired results, the child incorporates those constructive behaviors into his or her fulfillment strategy. When misbehaviors bring the desired results, those misbehaviors are incorporated into the child's fulfillment strategy. People may feel connected because they belong to the community or to a gang. People may feel capable of taking on responsibility or may make a career out of avoiding what is expected of them. People may feel that they count when they contribute or they may find their significance through misbehavior or self-elevation. Teen gangs and cults provide all the Crucial Cs through negative means, but for some people a gang is the only place where they feel that they are connected and capable and that they count. (See Crucial Cs chart in the Appendix.)

Each time children succeed in getting a need met, they gain in the courage available to sustain them through the next series of trials and errors they will experience as they strive to master the next task. When children experience only failure and don't succeed in getting their needs met sufficiently, they lose some of their courage and become increasingly timid in the face of new challenges.

If we want children to go about getting their needs met in constructive ways and to possess the courage they will need throughout their entire lives, we need to become aware of the part that we as parents and caregivers play in the results children get from their learning efforts. Criticism and disrespect interfere with children's desire and ability to develop the courage they need to get the Crucial Cs through constructive means.

Since every behavior has a purpose, one way to understand our children is to look for the underlying purposes of their actions. We do that in terms of the Crucial Cs, looking at all behavior as a result of—

- Feeling the Crucial Cs
- Striving to feel the Crucial Cs
- Not feeling one or more of the Crucial Cs

The goals of misbehavior

We must try to determine how our children see the world and their place in it. Keep in mind that children's behavior reveals a strategy to connect, feel capable, and count in the family. Problems arise because, as Rudolf Dreikurs said, "children are expert observers, but make many mistakes in interpreting what they observe. They often draw wrong conclusions and choose mistaken ways in which to find their place" (1964, p. 15).

Misbehavior is a symptom of these wrong conclusions. A child who is discouraged about his or her ability to connect, feel capable, and count through constructive means develops coping strategies designed to compensate for the missing Cs. These coping strategies, which include behaviors like quitting, avoiding, cheating, clowning, bullying, controlling, forgetting, stalling, denying, rationalizing, making excuses, blaming others, and being impulsive, fall into four general categories of short-range goals that Dreikurs called the "mistaken goals of behavior" (1964). These coping strategies, then, are actually the misguided behaviors used to pursue mistaken goals.

Children who don't feel **connected** feel insecure and isolated and might try to prove they belong by seeking **attention**.

Children who don't feel **capable** feel inadequate. If they can't feel competent in their own right, they may choose an alternative route, mistaking power for competency. They may seek this short-range goal of **power** by trying to control others or by showing that others can't control them.

Children who don't feel as if they **count** may try to punish others for their feeling of insignificance. They may try to get **revenge** and hurt back as they have felt hurt.

Finally, children without **courage** often feel inferior. They may use **avoidance** or assumed disability and give up in order to preserve the remnants of their damaged self-esteem.

The problem is that these goals are like candy; they provide quick satisfaction but have no long-term nourishing effect. Since they, like candy, seem to take care of the immediate discomfort, the child may not even bother to try for healthier relationships and the resultant damage may not be noticed until the damage is serious.

Instead of their trying to **connect** by seeking undue attention, we want children to experience belonging through **cooperation**. We want children to feel **capable** and competent through **self-reliance**, not from the misuse of power. We want children to feel that they **count** and can make a difference through **contribution,** not revenge! We want children to develop **resiliency** and have the **courage** to face and overcome their difficulties, not avoid them.

REMINDER: The misbehavior you see is not the problem. It's a solution to a problem the child experiences. We have to help children find alternative solutions.

Each of the goals can be pursued through active or passive behaviors. In the less constructive modes of behavior, children can try to get our attention by actions that are disruptive or by constantly getting us to remind them of their responsibilities. They may try to prove their power by trying to show others that "you can't stop me!" or by showing them that "you can't make me!" Children who are bent on revenge might show their pain by trying to hurt others or by trying to make others feel bad by showing how others have hurt them. Children may be so discouraged about their ability to measure up that their goal is to get us to give up on them. They may do this through hyperactive behavior or by overemphasizing their learning disabilities. Although a child may or may not be correctly labeled or diagnosed, not every child with such a diagnosis displays these inadequacies and gives up. We all know people who have developed strategies to compensate for these problems and have gone on to achieve great things. For example, Einstein was dyslexic, and we can only imagine what it would have been like to be Robin Williams's Mom and try to get him to sit still.

Why is the goal important?

If you go to a doctor complaining of a pain in your chest, you expect her to do an examination, determine the problem, and come up with a treatment plan that is appropriate to you. We all know that the same symptom can be present in different illnesses. A pain in the chest can be a sign of indigestion, pneumonia, a heart problem, anxiety, or other conditions. If we try to treat the symptom without deter-mining the underlying problem, we would be ineffective, at best; and at worst, we might cause even more damage.

Just like the doctor, if we want to effectively respond to a child's misbehavior we must first determine the underlying problem, not just react to the symptom. The same behavior may be used to pursue different goals. For example, a child may forget to come in on time because he wants you to remind him. He wants attention. Another child may forget to come in because she wants to show you that you can't make her do what you want. She wants to show her power. Another child may forget to come in so that you will worry. This child feels hurt and wants to get you back by getting revenge. And finally, a child may forget to come in because he doesn't feel capable of taking on any responsibility and he wants you to give up and stop expecting him to remember. This child is trying to protect his self-esteem by avoidance or display of inadequacy.

We all forget sometimes, and not every mistake is misbehavior. So, before we get overly concerned about mistaken goals and discouragement, we should ask ourselves the following questions:

1. Is this behavior repetitious or is it a one-time mistake?

2. How is the child responding to correction? Does the behavior continue or improve?
3. Could this behavior be the result of a developmental stage? Children go through many stages of development. Each stage brings with it new capabilities and new tasks. We should be aware of what constitutes age-appropriate behavior.
4. Could this behavior be the result of a medical problem? The first signs of some neurological and other physiological conditions (e.g., bladder problems, attention deficit disorder, hyperactivity, hearing loss, etc.) may be inappropriate behavior (bed-wetting, distractibility, rambunctiousness, not responding to others, etc.). This list is by no means comprehensive and any persistent problems should be evaluated by qualified professionals.
5. Is this a child whose style is different from yours? Each child is an individual; each child has his or her own personality and rate and style of development. We have to work with the child's style, not try to change it
6. Is the child copying adult behavior?
7. Is the behavior a simple mistake due to lack of training or information?
8. Are we expecting too much or too little given the child's age or capabilities?

If after asking ourselves these questions, we have concluded that the child's behavior is the result of discouragement, we can use the following clues to help us determine the child's mistaken goal:

• How do we feel when the child misbehaves?
• What is the child's response to correction?

If you feel. . .	And the child's response is. . .	The goal is to achieve . . .
irritated, annoyed	to temporarily stop	attention
angry, challenged	to escalate, to intensify	power
like punishing, or you feel hurt	to make self disliked, or to hurt	revenge
despair, hopeless	to display inadequacy	avoidance

By focusing on the discouragement of the child rather than on the symptomatic misbehavior, we can look for ways to motivate and encourage instead of looking for techniques to stop, control, or punish the child.

How does the child develop mistaken goals?

The four goals of misbehavior are mistaken approaches to trying to achieve the Crucial Cs. Children, using a process of trial and error, try to figure out ways to connect, feel capable, and count. They try different behaviors, keeping the ones that seem to work and discarding the others. Since they are both human and young, however, they are bound to make some mistakes.

The following scenarios use the same initial problem to illustrate the different behaviors that may occur when children pursue different mistaken goals. In each case, note the child's reaction to correction and the parent's feeling.

Mistaken goal #1: Seeking undue attention as a way to connect

Mother: "Tommy, please pick up your things."

Tommy: "Sure, Mom." He then hangs up his coat leaving his gloves, boots, and school bag on the floor.

Mother: "Tommy, you left all this other stuff on the floor. Please come get it."

Tommy then picks up the rest of his things but on the way to the closet gets distracted and begins to play with his toys.

Mom notices what he's doing and reminds him again to put his things away. Tommy says, "Okay," and finally puts the things away.

How would the parent feel? She would probably feel irritated and annoyed because so much reminding is required. Mom might be thinking, "It took so much effort to get him to do it; it would have been easier if I'd done it myself."

This most common mistaken goal arises when a child discovers that it feels good to get attention. The child may reason that getting attention is a good way to be sure of belonging, of being connected. At this critical point, children may get the mistaken idea that the only way to be sure of belonging is to keep others busy meeting their needs or at least not let others be busy with something or someone else. Such reasoning results in a demand for too much attention. Of course, we all need attention, but a demand for exclusive or full-time attention, though reasonable by the child's standards, is not realistic, appropriate, or acceptable by most parents' standards.

In an attempt to appease children who seek attention instead of constructive connection, adults often act as if attention were a cup that could be filled and expect that when it is full, the child will say, "Thanks, I've had enough. Why don't you go do your work now?" But this cup has a hole in the bottom. We can keep adding more, but we can't ever fill the cup. Children with the mistaken goal of getting attention never get "enough." They soon forget the attention they have already gotten because it's only the attention they *don't* get that is important to them. When the demand is total, nothing less will do.

Dealing with a child who is constantly seeking attention is like trying to have a serious conversation with someone who is wearing a funny hat and hopping around—it simply can't be done. The child's distracting behavior may start off as amusing to the parent, but the constant disruptions quickly become annoying and irritating.

When children disturb us with disruptive behavior, forget things, interrupt, and otherwise demand full attention, we usually do the wrong thing in response. We notice the misbehavior and may make the mistake of giving them the attention they demand. "I've told you sixteen times, you may not interrupt!" What has the child just done sixteen times? Interrupted us. And what have we just done sixteen times? Given the child undue attention.

What we want is for the child to learn that he or she is important even when we are busy doing something else. If the child feels securely connected, the child can find a way to belong through cooperation. The way to guide the child in that direction is to ignore the attention-demanding misbehavior and give attention to appropriate behavior.

As with all misbehaviors, the child's attention-seeking usually provokes negative feelings in the adult. We frequently are tempted to try to change children and convince them that their efforts are misguided, but in doing so, we only create defensiveness and may make matters worse. Instead, we need to change our response to the misbehavior. If we want to change our response, we have to address our negative feelings. To deal with the frustration and annoyance associated with attention-seeking behavior, it is helpful to imagine the child wearing a sign that says, "I want to connect. Catch me being good." Children remember and retain the behaviors that gain an adult's response; children abandon those behaviors to which adults don't respond.

Once we begin to understand children's behavior in a different way, we can change our responses. We can stop reinforcing mistaken goals and begin to guide the child to more constructive approaches for connecting to others. The basic principle is to modify our response to the child's behavior based on an understanding of the child's goal. Here are some effective strategies for redirecting children's behaviors:

1. **Minimize the attention given to misbehavior.** We don't have to notice every slight transgression. Remember that children repeat behaviors that get the desired response. Children who are driven by the desire for attention would rather be reprimanded than ignored.

2. **Notice the behaviors you want to encourage.** Focus on contributions, working well with others, cooperation, and other constructive behaviors.

3. **Act *before* there is a problem.** We are often tempted to leave children alone when they are playing "nicely" and only step in when there is a problem. However logical this approach may seem, it doesn't work. It misses the

opportunities to recognize and appreciate constructive behavior and reinforces the idea that misbehavior gets attention. Instead, we should give children attention when they are not demanding it.

4. **Act, don't talk!** When we spend too much time talking, children quickly learn to tune us out. Instead of reminding the children to come in for dinner, call them once and then serve the meal. If they come in late, their dinner will be cold.

5. **Give jobs that get positive attention by being helpful to others** such as answering the telephone and serving the dessert. In this way, we can redirect children towards cooperative behavior.

To illustrate the use of strategies 1, 3, and 4, for example, we return to the dialogue between Tommy and his mother. What can the parent do to ensure that a conflict such as Tommy's and Mom's does not arise again? Suppose Mom finds a calm moment and engages Tommy in making an agreement about when and how things should be put away. A logical start is a great prevention tool. By discussing who should do what, by when, and how *before* there is a problem, parents can choose a time for teaching when the child is receptive and avoid many conflicts.

In this case, if Mom and Tommy agree that he will put all of his things in the closet before he watches television, when he doesn't do it, she can say, "Tommy, remember our agreement. Please put your things away." If Tommy continues his stalling behavior, Mom can simply turn off the TV, saying, "You may turn it back on when you have done what you agreed to do." It is important that Mom doesn't do any more talking or reminding. Since Tommy's behavior is an example of seeking undue attention, he will probably try to engage her in some way. But when he realizes that he can't draw her in, he will put his things away. If Tommy adamantly refuses, the goal he is seeking is probably power, not attention.

Mother should also remember to make time for positive connection. She could occasionally watch television with Tommy and discuss what he likes about the programs, how he feels about different characters, their behaviors, and choices, etc. She might suggest they read a book on a similar topic and compare the way characters and situations are presented. Having joined Tommy in an activity that he enjoys, she can invite him to join her in other activities.

As noted in tips 2 and 5, Mom should comment on behaviors that she wants to encourage. While it is important to let children learn to play on their own, it is also important to give attention when it is not demanded. From time to time Mom could ask Tommy if she could join him when he is busy with a project saying, "That looks like fun, do you want some company?"

Mistaken goal #2: Seeking power as a way to feel capable

Father: "Marissa, please pick up your things."

Marissa ignores Dad.

Father: "Marissa, I told you to pick up your things."

Marissa: "Later, I'm busy."

Father: "Marissa, we had an agreement that you'd put your things away before you got involved with something else."

Marissa: "I don't remember any agreement."

The reminder has escalated from a simple request into a full-blown argument. Instead of gaining Marissa's cooperation, Dad is now fighting about who is right and who is wrong.

How would the parent feel? He would probably feel angry or challenged because no matter how logical the request, there is always resistance. Dad might be thinking, "All we ever seem to do is fight, why can't she ever just do what she is told?"

Children have many years to try out ways to become capable of caring for themselves, but self-reliance is not always the result of their efforts. When children compare themselves to parents or older siblings, for example, they may not realize that they will grow and develop their own competencies. They may decide that they don't measure up and are in an inferior position. The child may try to compensate for the feeling of powerlessness by trying to be "more powerful" than others.

The first signs of the power goal may show up as the "terrible two's." When the child first begins to experience the power of language and the word "no," the child practices it at every opportunity. If parents respond to these first signs of autonomy by trying to *force* the child to cooperate, he may become convinced that important people in this world are able to make others do as they say. If the child doesn't feel successful at bossing others, he can at least show them that they can't boss him. What is more powerful than defeating the most powerful people in your life?

Since everyone wants to feel "empowered" in some way, when we don't provide children with the opportunity to develop their competencies and become self-reliant, they may get the wrong idea about being "powerful." We all want our children to become responsible and to feel capable, but in our haste to get things done it may seem easier to do things for them than to take the time to teach them how to be responsible for themselves. It may be tempting to remind children of their obligations and tell them what to do and how to do it, but it doesn't encourage self-reliance.

Living with a child who is seeking power is like trying to have a relationship with someone who only wants to fight with you or defeat you. We are usually tempted to do the wrong thing in response to his constant challenges. We get so angry at this child that we want to "show him that he can't get away with this!" Of course, what we are actually doing is impressing the child with *our* power and showing him that he may need to work even harder to defeat us. He may decide to go undercover and resist passively, by forgetting, not listening, or failing at school. He may become incorrigible; or he may pick on those who are smaller or weaker.

What we should do in this situation is what Rudolf Dreikurs suggested: instead of trying to take the wind out of his sail, we should take our sail out of his wind (1964, p. 155). He can keep on blowing but we will not be pushed around. In this way, we show the child that we *refuse to fight* with him, and we *refuse to give in* to his unreasonable demands.

To counteract feelings of anger when you find yourself feeling challenged by a child, try to imagine the child wearing a sign that says: "I want to be capable. Involve me and give me choices."

Understanding the child's display of power in a different way can help to neutralize our anger and enable us to change our responses. We can stop reinforcing this mistaken goal and begin to guide the child to more constructive approaches for feeling capable. Here are some effective strategies for redirecting children's behaviors towards seeking to develop their competence:

1. **Think about what *you* can do rather then what *they* should do.**

2. **When correcting a misbehaving child, focus on the behavior, not the child.** While a child's actions may be unacceptable, the child never is.

3. **Don't escalate.** Refuse to be drawn into a struggle for power. If you fight with the child, he or she may decide to resist in order to save face.

4. **Give this child real responsibilities to let him or her know that you think that the child is capable.** Remember to give choices and involve the child in decision making. In this way the child becomes empowered through constructive means.

5. **Whenever possible decide on rules and consequences as a family.** In this way you can avoid being set up as the authority to be defeated. If anyone breaks an agreed-upon rule, it is the family the person is challenging. This consensus is especially helpful to prevent a parent and child from getting into a standoff.

Just as with Tommy, the situation with Marissa can be handled with a logical start. It is especially important with a child who is seeking power that the parent and child decide beforehand on what will happen if the agreement is broken by either parent or child. This method of developing fail-safe agreements is respectful to everyone involved. It sets the stage for teaching through consequences and avoids escalating the power struggle into a cycle of punishment and revenge.

One example of a fail-safe agreement in Marissa's situation would be that Dad would agree to avoid disrespecting Marissa with constant nagging and reminding and Marissa would agree to take care of her job before dinner. They would also have to agree on the fail-safe. For example, if Dad forgets and starts reminding, he would have to put away Marissa's things. If Marissa sits down to dinner with her job undone, she would find her empty plate turned upside down as a friendly reminder to fulfill her agreement before she begins to eat. The reason this solution should work is that Marissa is included in the problem-solving. She does not need to resist in order to feel empowered. If she turns her plate over and begins to eat, it could mean that she feels coerced or is trying to test Dad's promise to avoid disrespect and punishment. If this happens, Dad should avoid being drawn into a fight. He should say nothing at this time. After dinner Dad can say to Marissa, "I noticed that you decided to ignore our agreement. I'd like to understand why and see if we can't come up with a solution that you are willing to stick with."

Mistaken goal #3: Seeking revenge as a way to count

Mother: "Clark, please pick up your things."

Clark doesn't respond.

Mother: "Clark, did you hear me?"

Clark: "Yeah, yeah, I heard you."

Mother: "Then why didn't you answer me?"

Clark: "Cause, I'm tired of you nagging me all the time."

Mother: "I'm not nagging you, I'm only trying to get you to stick to your agreement. Now get to it."

Clark: "That's not fair. I have to agree with you just to get you off my back. You never bug Dad, you pick his things up."

Mother: "That's different. Your father works hard and does plenty of other things. You only think about yourself."

Clark: "You always notice what other people do right but you only notice what I do wrong. I hate you!"

Mother: "Don't speak to me like that, young man. Go to your room until you change your attitude."

The initial request has turned into a hurtful exchange. The goal is no longer cooperation or even winning the argument—it is proving that the other person is bad.

How would the parent feel? She would probably feel attacked, angry, and hurt. She would be tempted to punish. She might be thinking, "How did things get so bad? There's no way to get through to him."

In our society, there is little chance for a child to make a useful contribution. In earlier times, it was important that each person do his part. Everyone's survival depended on it; if you didn't bring in the wood there was no heat; if you forgot to gather the eggs there was no breakfast. Today, we give children jobs with little status, like taking out the garbage, and when they forget we nag and remind them, and often do the job ourselves. Even such personal responsibilities as doing homework, taking lunch money, and remembering books often become the parent's job. It is little wonder that kids don't see their contributions as important, and often believe that adults' requests for cooperation are simply arbitrary means for controlling them.

If a child becomes so discouraged that she feels that she is not needed, cannot be liked or get her way, she may move to the goal of revenge. When a child becomes motivated by revenge, she has come to believe that her only chance to prove that she counts is by hurting others as she has felt hurt.

Revenge-seeking behavior is often observed in children who have been neglected, abused, or overpowered. Also, revenge is often a response of a pampered child as well. Pampering convinces a child that she has a right to special attention and when she doesn't get it, she has the right to punish those who deprived her of her "birthright."

A child who resorts to revenge is one of the most difficult to work with. She will often push until a parent gets mad or upset and the child says, "See, I knew you didn't like me." Parents may think that a little more attention will turn this child around, but the more the parent gives, the more the child escalates until the parent gives up in frustrated anger and hurt. Living with a child seeking revenge is like living with someone who is covered with mouse traps that are always baited, ready to catch you before you can hurt her.

Before you can figure out what to do, you must realize that the child's goal is to prove that the world is unfair and that she wants to punish others for the injustice that she suffers. The first step in dealing with revenge is to try to rebuild the relationship. However, parents must act swiftly to maintain their self-respect, and protect their own rights while not humiliating the child or infringing on the child's rights.

Adults who are confronted with a child who is trying to hurt them are tempted to hurt back and punish. One way to keep from getting caught up in the cycle of revenge is to remind yourself of the child's great pain and discouragement. It is sometimes helpful to imagine the child wearing a sign that says: "I want to count. Find something to like about me. I'm hurting."

Before trying any strategies with a child seeking revenge, it is critical to build a relationship, which will not be easy as the child's goal is to prove that you do not care. To help fight our own discouragement it is important to remember that the goal of relationship building underlies all of the suggested strategies. Although we may be tempted to show the child how bad she is, this is not necessary. She is already convinced that others feel this way. Our job is to convince the discouraged child otherwise and to get her to believe in herself.

One way to help a discouraged child develop her courage is to enlist the aid of other family members and friends. Explain that she is very discouraged and you would like their help in encouraging her. Ask people to go out of their way to make some positive comment or connection with her. Warn them that she may sabotage their efforts. You may have to brainstorm together to find the hidden good beneath her obvious misbehavior.

Even with the most supportive friends and family, you may decide this child is so discouraged that you will want to seek professional help. Although one child may be the focus of your concern, the whole family is always affected. The most effective way to have an impact is to involve everyone in family counseling.

Our own hurt feelings become more bearable once we are able to see the child's deep discouragement. If we can put her hurtful behavior into context, then we can stop reinforcing her mistaken perceptions. Only then can we begin to guide the child to more constructive approaches for feeling that she counts. Some effective strategies include

1. **Make a list of positives about this child** and refer to it often, especially when you're feeling defeated. Share the list with others and ask them to contribute to it.

2. **Refuse to retaliate, escalate, or humiliate**. Maintain a respectful relationship. Remove yourself, before you get angry. Allow the child to experience the natural consequences of his or her behavior.

3. **Before trying to resolve conflicts, allow for a cooling off period** to remind yourself that this child who is hurting you is actually feeling hurt herself.

4. This child knows injustice, and will often be willing to help those less fortunate. **Offer many chances to help others,** and let the child know that his or her contributions are necessary.

5. **Share responsibility for solving problems**. Ask the child, "What do you think we should do about this situation?"

Although we would expect that Clark would not keep to his agreement, we would have to initiate logical starts and fail-safes anyway because we have to begin to establish a respectful relationship. All of the above tips are very important here. Mom could make a date to talk with Clark later; she could decide to work on the relationship for a week before she brings up any problems; she could invite him to work with her on projects (allowing him to say no with no repercussions); and she should eliminate criticism and focus on what Clark does right. Until Clark's perception of his situation changes and until the parents' perception of Clark becomes more hopeful, no progress is possible.

Mistaken goal #4: Using avoidance to compensate for loss of courage.

Father: "Georgia, please pick up your things."
Georgia picks up a couple of her things, drops one, goes to pick it up and drops two more. She starts to cry.

Father: "What's the matter? There's nothing to cry about, honey. Just take one thing at a time."

Georgia takes her coat to the closet but can't get it to stay on the hanger. She begins to cry again.

Father: "Look dear, watch me" Father patiently demonstrates for the third time this week how to hang up a coat. Then he asks her to get her boots.

Georgia returns upset and says, "I could only find one boot."

How would the parent feel? He would probably feel like giving up. He might be thinking, "What's the use? She can't seem to do even the simplest tasks. Nothing I do seems to help. It's hopeless."

Although the initial requests are the same in all of the preceding examples, the children's responses to correction and the parents' feelings are different because each child's goal is different.

This last goal has been called "avoidance of failure" and "displayed or assumed inadequacy." It describes the child who is convinced that she cannot succeed and cannot have power. She decides that her best chance to preserve her self-esteem is to get others to give up on her; at least this way she avoids situations where she might be humiliated. This child's goal is to be left alone to suffer in private, and to daydream about what might have been. She may think, "I'd prefer you think I am stupid rather than give you proof that I am." This is a child who has opted out. The adult's task is to enable the child.

This child may slip into the background and may be overlooked. She may even be labeled hyperactive or learning disabled. Whether or not the diagnosis is correct is less important than the feelings of hopelessness that are elicited in the people who interact with her. Parents and teachers, discouraged about any possibility of improvement, often give up trying to get her involved. Professional help is often necessary to help counteract the despair of both the child and the parent. It is essential that this child have someone in her life who refuses to give up hope.

With a child struggling to preserve self-esteem, we must focus intensively on encouragement. She must be convinced that the real world is better than the world of daydreams. It's awfully lonely in that world. We must try to give her a sense of belonging, show her that she is liked and that she has something valuable to offer. By experiencing success, this child begins to get the courage to try again.

Keep in mind that failure to accomplish usually comes from fear of failure, not laziness. And when you find yourself feeling hopeless and discouraged, try to imagine this child wearing a sign that says: "Develop my courage. Believe in me. Don't give up."

Discouraged children usually come with discouraged parents. Developing a manageable plan will be encouraging to both. Here are some strategies for building courage.

1. **Make mistakes a learning experience.** Point out that one must risk failure in order to develop new skills. Ask, "What will you do differently next time?" Be sure to accept your own mistakes. In order to demonstrate the importance of perseverance and learning from experience, share stories about people the child knows who have recovered from mistakes.

2. **Create situations where success is probable.** Divide larger tasks into many more manageable steps with benchmarks to reflect progress. Provide an encouraging tutor if necessary.

3. **Recognize any effort or small improvement.** Make sure this applies to everyone in the family and not just this child. We sometimes only acknowledge perfection. This is only encouraging to those who consistently do superior work. Those who don't feel they will be successful may give up altogether. By focusing on improvement for everyone, we make it clear that effort is important.

4. **Teach positive self-talk**. Listen to these children and what they are saying about themselves. Don't allow them to discourage themselves further with negative statements. If you hear them say, "I can't," encourage them to change it to, "I haven't learned how to do this yet." If the child says, "I'm stupid," separate the person from what he or she does. Respond with, "Making mistakes doesn't mean you're stupid. Making mistakes means you're trying and learning."

5. **Don't give up.**

In the case of Georgia, Dad could anticipate problems before they arise. He might set up the closet with an easy-to-reach hook, a box labeled "boots," and a convenient shelf for her other things. He could meet her at the door and help her with her tasks, making sure that he doesn't do the jobs for her. In this way he would be following the four steps for guiding the child from dependence to independence:

1. First, we do the job for the child.

2. Next we do the job with the child assisting.

3. Then the child does the job with our assistance.

4. Finally, the child does the job independently.

Developing Self-Esteem through Encouragement

Most of us have been surprised when we meet people who have achieved a lot in their lives but still have low self-esteem. We are even more surprised when we meet people who start off with the odds against them but persevere, convinced that they will get to where they want to be. Many people think self-esteem is determined by the difference between the self-ideal (how I think I should be) and the self-image (how I think I am). The true measure of people's self-esteem, however, is related to their self-confidence about their ability to bridge the gap and achieve their goals. Self-esteem is based on the conclusions that individuals develop about their sense of competence and worth, about their abilities to make a difference and to meet and overcome challenges, to learn from both success and failure, and to view themselves and others with dignity and respect. Children listen to what we say and watch what we do and come to conclusions about what they *should* be like and how they *really* are. In order to increase the likelihood that we can positively influence a child's self-esteem, motivation, and courage, we must develop the art of encouragement.

Encouragement versus evaluative praise

Encouragement means to instill courage by helping people see their strengths and develop belief in themselves. High self-esteem is related to the belief that if we work hard and keep trying we will develop the skills we need to feel successful. Although experts often extol the value of using praise to raise children's self-esteem, praise frequently has the opposite effect. Commenting on improvement and effort is more encouraging than only noticing when a job is successfully completed. When we praise, we are usually pointing out what we think someone already does well. There are several problems with this kind of praise.

1. By our focusing primarily on what our children already do well, they may get the idea that success is the most important value. They may decide to avoid working in any area where success is not already guaranteed.

Success, however, is usually dependent upon the willingness to put forth the effort needed to improve.

2. When we focus on what we think rather than encouraging self-evaluation, we may actually be teaching our children to become dependent on others' opinions. While we may like the idea that young children try to please us, we usually worry when we see teenagers overly concerned with gaining the approval of their friends.

3. The child may interpret the absence of praise as proof of not being good enough.

Encouragement helps people accept imperfection and remain "try-ers."

Encouragement	**Evaluative Praise**
an attitude	a verbal reward
task/situation-centered	person-centered
emphasizes effort and improvement	earned by being superior
may be given during task	job must be well done/completed
shows acceptance	is judgmental
fosters independence	fosters dependence
emphasizes self-evaluation	emphasizes others' opinions
develops self-esteem	develops self-consciousness

Helping Children to Feel the Crucial Cs

The best way to encourage children and develop their self-esteem is by helping them to feel the Crucial Cs through constructive means. Below, in outline form, are some useful tips.

Helping the child to feel connected

1. Provide many opportunities for cooperative interaction.
    A. Develop family rules and problem solve at family meetings.
    B. Play games cooperatively. Helping should not be seen as cheating (there are many cooperative games on the market and games like Scrabble can be easily converted). Engage in singing and playing music together, working around the house and yard, and other such group activities and projects.
    C. Take turns with different members together planning an outing or surprise for the whole family.
    D. Develop a family identity. Talk about what your family is like, what you have in common.
    E. Engage in cooperative learning activities. Research an upcoming trip, learn about an area of the world, adopt a fish at the aquarium and then study and visit it, volunteer together for pledge walks for a valued cause, etc.

2. Give positive attention.
    A. Make time to spend with each child individually at some regular interval (this will depend on the age and interest of each child).
    B. If a child wants your attention and you are busy, arrange a time to talk.

C. Acknowledge each child's special skills and hobbies. Ask each child to share and teach other family members. Display everyone's work, not just perfect papers.

D. Don't make comparisons with other children.

E. Acknowledge children's moods ("Looks like you're having a hard day. Want to talk about it?" "You look awfully pleased today. What's up?")

3. Find and recognize strengths and talents.
   A. Look for strengths, not just academic, but also mechanical, artistic, athletic, creative, social.
   B. Be a talent scout. Find something the child is good at and uncover the skills used in that activity. Then show how these qualities are used in other areas. For example, what does it take to be good in math? Logic, some memorization, concentration, practice, stick-to-itiveness, being a good detective. These same skills are evident in many strategy games, athletics, and other hobbies.
   C. As the old song suggests, "Accentuate the Positive, Eliminate the Negative."

4. Show acceptance: Separate the deed from the doer.
   A. Do so with both positive and negative behaviors.
   B. Be specific: "I liked the way you handled _____."
      "I liked it when you _____ because _____."
      When you _____, I felt _____ because _____."

5. Hold family meetings regularly.

Helping the child feel capable

1. Make each mistake a learning experience.
    A. Demonstrate learning from mistakes. Ask, "What did you learn from it?" and "What will you do differently next time?"
    B. Follow Piaget's advice. Look for logic behind an answer. Be more interested in why a child answers the way he or she does (it may be incorrect but it is rarely illogical.) "How did you come up with this?" "What did you think that I meant?" "What would you have said if you thought I meant _____?" "When you did that, what did you think would happen?" "Did you learn anything new or surprising?" "What will you do next time?"
    C. Note the way you respond to errors. Allowing children time to try again, offering clues, and suggesting alternatives convey that errors are a part of the learning process.
    D. Look for analytical ability, critical thinking, good judgment, effort, improvement, how far the person has come, not how far he or she has to go.
    E. Concentrate on the effort, not the errors. We need to be willing to accept mistakes if we want children to risk trying new things. Creative ideas are often built on a so-called mistake.
    F. Set the tone in the family: At the family meeting, ask, "Who worries about making a mistake or saying something wrong sometimes? If someone makes a mistake, what should we do? Do you think we should make fun of each other when we do make a mistake?"

2. Build confidence.
    A. Focus on improvement not perfection.
    B. Notice contributions.

    C. Build on strengths.
    D. Believe in the children.
       (1) Have realistic expectations of them.
       (2) Allow them to struggle and succeed if the job is within their capabilities. Don't feel sorry for them or rescue them from a manageable problem. Both are disrespectful and discouraging. You can, however, acknowledge the difficulty of the situation.
       (3) Focus on the present, not the past (don't expect repetition of old behaviors) or the future (kids worry about their ability to measure up).
    E. Analyze successes to see what they did right. Why was it successful? Would they be willing to teach others?
    F. Ensure successes. Divide up large tasks into smaller, more manageable ones. Give opportunities to repeat successful experiences.

3. Hold family meetings regularly.

Helping the child feel he or she counts

1. Through contribution.
    A. By helping the family.
       (1) Offer jobs that are meaningful. Give positions of responsibility.
       (2) Provide choices of jobs. Brainstorm:
          (a) What could we do?
          (b) What do we need to do it?
          (c) How can we get what we need?
          (d) Who can do what part?
       (3) Invite input into scheduling (e.g., When should we do our jobs? Go on an outing?).

        (4) Make rules together. Discuss different types.
            (a) Rules that cover behaviors that make being here easy and fun.
            (b) Rules that cover behaviors that sabotage or interfere with others' rights to play, participate, learn, or feel safe.

   B. By helping each other.
      (1) Teach each other skills.
         (a) Make a list of "skills I am willing to teach" and "things I would like to learn."
         (b) Brainstorm what kids would like to learn: knitting, clay, jump rope, basketball, etc.
         (c) Ask or identify who is good at specific skills. A parent can encourage a discouraged child by identifying a valuable talent.
      (2) Helping each other solve problems at family meetings.

   C. By helping in the community.
      (1) With charity drives, neighborhood cleanup projects, etc.
      (2) Regular visits to nursing homes, volunteering at shelters.
      (3) Tutoring younger children.

2. Through recognition.
   A. Set up an "I Can" box. Have kids fill out cards on something they did that they are proud of or something they recently learned or something positive they noticed about someone else. Share these cards at family meeting.
   B. Have friendly discussions where family members periodically evaluate themselves, develop and discuss goals, and assess improvement. Make sure that this is a time for self-evaluation, not criticism.

C. Give appreciations and compliments at family meetings.

3. Hold family meetings regularly.

Helping the child develop courage

1. Have the courage to be imperfect. Don't expect perfection of self or others.

2. Point to strengths, not weaknesses.

3. Don't make comparisons with others.

4. Ask questions (Do you understand? Do you need help? Is this what you meant?) in order to—
   A. Encourage active participation.
   B. See if their understanding is the same as yours.
   C. Learn where help and/or correction are necessary.

5. Ask yourself the following questions:
   A. Am I inspiring self-evaluation or dependence on others' evaluation?
   B. Am I respectful or patronizing?
   C. Am I seeing the child's point of view or only my own?
   D. Would I say this to a friend?

6. Avoid debilitating help.
   A. Don't overlook misbehavior. Don't avoid taking appropriate action.
   B. Don't regularly do for children what the children can do for themselves.
   C. Don't rescue kids from uncomfortable consequences of their actions. (Of course, we have to intervene

whenever a situation is dangerous or if the outcome would be extreme discouragement, but discomfort isn't dangerous!)

7. Avoid criticism.
   A. People often become defensive when they feel criticized. If you want someone to hear what you say you must already have a very secure relationship (and even then, it's tough).
   B. Check out what children are asking for. Is it encouragement or correction? Do they want you to give feedback on ideas or presentation? Are they asking if there are stains on their shirts, or are they asking if you like their outfits?

8. Hold family meetings regularly.

Using Logical Discipline to Teach the Logic of the Social Order

Parents have an obligation to educate children to become responsible citizens. Children need to learn that true freedom can only exist within a social order. Rudolf Dreikurs said, "Freedom is part of democracy; but the subtle point that we cannot have freedom unless we respect the freedom of others is seldom recognized...In order for everyone to have freedom, we must have order and order bears with it certain restrictions and obligations. Freedom also implies responsibility" (1964, p. 9). Without certain limits no one can feel secure and without the opportunity for choice no one can feel free. Imagine how frightening it would be to cross the Golden Gate Bridge if it had no guardrails. Although we try not to bump into the railing, we feel secure knowing that it is there.

Consequences versus punishment

Since we can't protect our children from life directly, we must try to teach them to deal with it effectively. We must give them the opportunity to experience the consequences of their actions and to learn from their mistakes. Lecturing and warnings only turn kids off and make them think that the only danger to avoid is being stuck in a room with a "nagging " adult.

Punishment too can backfire. When we arbitrarily apply an unconnected punishment, we run the risk of interfering with the learning process. The child may be so angered, hurt, or distracted by our reaction that he or she misses the real lesson; that his or her misbehavior is inappropriate, dangerous, or ineffective. This child may learn instead that he or she shouldn't misbehave because it gets us mad or that misbehavior is okay as long as you don't get caught.

Think of a time when you really got into trouble. What do you remember about it? Most people remember more about the punishment or the unreasonableness of their parents' reaction than they do about what they did wrong. The lesson children learn should always underscore the connection between their behavior and its results.

It is helpful to make a distinction between punishment and logical consequences in order to maintain the connection between behavior and its results. Punishment is an arbitrary consequence, designed to teach through discomfort or pain, either physical or psychological. It is based on the assumption that children learn best by **suffering** the consequences of their behavior. The approach of logical consequences, on the other hand, works under the assumption that children learn best by **experiencing** the results of their behavior.

This doesn't mean that we allow our children to stumble into dangerous situations. We must always keep safety first, but whenever possible, the parent should step back or arrange situations so that the child experiences reality.

Respectful guidance allows children to experience safely the natural and logical consequences of their behavior, whether they are positive or negative.

The major differences between consequences and punishment

	Punishment	Logical Consequences
Teaches	Arbitrary power, external control	Cooperation, self-discipline
Adult's emotion	Anger	Friendly, concerned
Adult's action is	Hurting, arbitrary, often impulsive	Seeking agreement, related to behavior, thoughtful, deliberate
Adult's focus is	On the past (what happened), on what CAN'T be done	On the future (what needs to be done) on what CAN be done
Child feels	Belittled, inferior	Capable, respected
Child remembers	Injustice, humiliation	Personal contribution, connection between behavior and results
Purpose	Control over others	Self-control

A logical consequence must pass the test of the "3 Rs." It should be

1. **related** logically to the misbehavior;
2. **respectful** in order to avoid any humiliation, and to be both firm (to show respect for self) and kind (to show respect for the child); and
3. **reasonable** so that it is as logically understandable to the child as to the adult. An overly harsh or angry consequence is always perceived as a punishment.

The object of discipline is to learn self-discipline, to guide one towards self-control, to help the child see what should be and what should not be done, and to take responsibility for whichever direction is taken.

On the subject of hitting

Phyllis Harrison-Ross, co-author of *The Black Child: A Parent's Guide* (1973), says, "The aim of discipline is not to make the child afraid of the parent. It's to teach the child how to live so that he gets the most out of his own life, so he doesn't infringe on the rights of others, so that he is a valuable person, both to himself and to others."

We should not continue to confuse discipline with punishment. Punishment always involves pain. Discipline sometimes involves some inconvenience, but pain is not a way to teach.

Children who are consistently punished or spanked may not learn that they did something wrong; but they may learn that there is something wrong with them. Furthermore, punishment doesn't teach children what they should do instead.

If kids don't learn what they should be doing instead, misbehavior is likely to continue and to invite more punishment. This constant cycle will result in the low self-esteem and poor self-image that we are trying to avoid. Children want to **connect** with their parents. They need the security that comes from this sense of connection in order to develop the confidence and courage they need to go forward and face life.

Hitting doesn't instill confidence or courage. It is humiliating and teaches fear. It provokes a poor self-concept, desire for revenge, and the idea that it is okay to hit the ones you love. Nobody ever feels good after being hit but instead might even feel worthless, as if he or she doesn't **count**.

Hitting is also likely to make children want revenge. If they can't take us on directly they may take it out on someone or something else or they may try lying, stealing, or being slow and forgetful. Social science research makes it clear that the most aggressive children are those who have been most punished.

Finally, when we hit we are modeling negative behavior. We succeed only in teaching that violent acts are a way to let off anger or it is acceptable to hit people to "teach them a lesson."

Stephen J. Bavolek, in his handbook, *Shaking, Hitting, Spanking: What to Do Instead*, warns of the dangers of corporal punishment. His discussion, adapted here, includes some common myths and rationales:

1. **Myth**: Some parents say that hitting is an act of love done to teach children what is good for them.

Fact: If such practices continue children may learn that it is all right to hit as long as you love, or that hitting is a sign of love. Both ideas may lead to abusive intimate relationships later on.

2. **Myth**: Physical punishment prepares children for the real world. Some people believe that, since the real world is filled with violence, we must toughen kids up to prepare them for it.

   Fact: Children first learn about the world and what is expected of them in their homes. That is where they make decisions about themselves and their ability to face the challenges they will meet. If the child is prepared with violence, the child will bring that into the outside world and transmit it to the neighborhood. "The real world would become less violent if violence in the home stopped" (p. 5).

3. **Myth**: "Infants need to be spanked because they don't understand language" (p. 6).

   Fact: Hitting an infant is always dangerous. "A young infant is too fragile to withstand any force" (p. 6). Although infants can't talk, they can learn. They learn from gestures, touch, expressions, and tone of voice.

4. **Myth**: "It's okay to hit as long as you aren't angry" (p. 6).

   Fact: There are more effective ways to teach children without doing damage to the child's self-esteem or the parent-child relationship. "If parents are not angry any more and have calmed down and are in control, why spank?" (p. 6).

5. **Myth**: "Children who aren't spanked become spoiled"
   (p. 5). Parents who depend on spanking and punishing
   to teach their children right from wrong may worry they
   will be left without any discipline techniques if hitting
   is eliminated. They worry that their children will be out
   of control.

   Fact: If we want children to become responsible and
   self-disciplined, we must use techniques that teach them
   to think, not simply react out of FEAR!

CAUTION: Logical consequences are so effective that
parents run the risk of overusing them. We often focus too
much on treating the symptom, in this case misbehavior,
and forget about curing the disease, low self-esteem and
discouragement. The result is that new symptoms keep
cropping up, and we spend our time and energy applying
bandages and doing cosmetic surgery.

It is important to remember that the value of consequences
goes beyond merely solving conflicts with our children.
Their intended purpose is to help guide and direct our
children to the path of responsibility and caring.
When children misbehave, our first job is to uncover the
underlying reasons for the behavior. If we determine that the
behavior is a result of discouragement and pursuing
mistaken goals, our first concern should be to develop a plan
for encouragement. We should concentrate on building a
relationship, creating an atmosphere of mutual respect, and
providing opportunities for experiencing the Crucial Cs.

Preparing Children to Live in a Democracy

If we want our children to become responsible citizens, we must help them to see themselves as capable, contributing members of society. Not only do they need to feel the Crucial Cs, but they also have to develop the essential skills of communication, self-discipline, responsibility, and good judgment.

Family meetings are the best way we know to teach social logic and democratic principles. In the family meeting, parents become strong, capable role models who do not use force or coercion to lead or guide the group. An effective family meeting gives children a chance to learn first-hand, through experience and observation, all of the perceptions, skills, and abilities that they need to develop the Crucial Cs through useful means.

Family meetings serve the needs of children to feel the Crucial Cs, develop essential skills, and live their lives meaningfully and constructively, including becoming well functioning members of a democratic society in the following ways.

Connect.   Meetings provide a strong sense of "family." This is our group. We need all of our members. Each child is guaranteed acceptance, a chance to be heard, and taken seriously. We start off the meeting with "compliments." We say thank you to each individual for something that was done during the past week. Everyone learns how to compliment and appreciate others and it feels good. This feeling invites participation, cooperation, and a sense that "we're in this together." Children learn that they belong.

Capable. Compliments, appreciations, problem-solving, and decision-making components of the meeting point out strengths and help all children see that they are competent. Everyone participates and sees personal resources that lead to solving problems. The child sees that there is *no magic*, that we have to *make* it happen, that we have to recognize the situation and what it requires, and that we have to share the responsibility for seeing that the solution we select is best for everyone.

Count. Children can see that what they do makes a difference and that they are capable of making necessary contributions. We need the ideas of all members in order to reach a solution that affects all of us.

Courage. Through problem-solving and evaluating outcomes, children learn that they can discuss their problems openly, learn from their mistakes, and try again.

Communication. We develop the ability and the mastery of conversation. Everyone is given a chance to speak and to be heard. Children are taught how to listen and they learn to respect others by not interrupting. We share ideas and feelings; we empathize with the situations of other members; and we negotiate until we reach agreements that all can accept. We don't vote; rather, we reach consensus. We don't want to divide into voting factions; we look for ways to develop a cooperative unit; and we do that through open communication. All are free to speak and all have an obligation to listen. Kids love it, especially the smaller ones.

Through this open dialogue process, we get to hear the perceptions that our children are developing. We are more likely to be able to influence their perceptions when we know what they are.

Self-discipline. We have to make sense of our behavior, our feelings, and our emotions. We learn how to develop strategies to reach the goals we set, and we take care to go about this without hurting others. We learn self-discipline by taking turns at listening and speaking, and we rotate the leader and the note-taker each week. We evaluate our own suggestions and the suggestions of other members; we decide how each might affect us; and we try to anticipate what we can learn from the decision we are considering. Each member gets to experience the consequences of his or her and the family's decisions and actions.

Responsibility. Everyone is given a chance to contribute to the family. All children are asked to take a turn leading meetings, taking notes of the proceedings, and participating in non-leadership roles. We recognize problems or concerns within the family; we share responsibility for offering solutions and doing the work that's needed; and we work to develop the willingness to make whatever changes are necessary.

We teach through natural and logical consequences and the kids are able to connect the results they get with decisions and choices they have helped to make. Most families find that when everyone has a say in setting the rules, they all have a stake in seeing that those rules are followed. We can't teach these ideas through punishment. Kids don't learn in a threatening environment.

Good judgment. We know good judgment is not developed through experience alone because everyone has had experiences but not everyone has good judgment. We use the family meeting to help children understand their and our experiences, to sort out what is significant, what they learned from their experiences, and what they and we will do differently as a result of our learning.

All of us together try out various proposed solutions and examine them to see how they will affect each of us and to determine if they are respectful of self and others. In these trial runs, we develop choices and work through their consequences.

Family Meeting Guidelines
(Excerpted from *Raising Kids Who Can,*
Bettner and Lew, Connexions Press, 1996).

1. A specific time and day of the week should be scheduled for the meeting.

In order to affirm the importance of the family meeting, no change is allowed without the consent of all members. This helps to make the meeting an integral part of the family routine.

Some busy families with ever-changing commitments find it difficult to meet on the same day each week. One solution to this dilemma is to add "choosing next meeting date" as a regular item on the agenda.

HINT: Parents should show how important the family is to them by not taking telephone calls or allowing themselves to be interrupted during this "important meeting."

2. Everyone's attendance is encouraged but not required.

Every member is expected to come since each one is an important part of the family. However, no one is forced to come since coercion invites resistance and rebellion. No one is forced to leave the meeting since that would be disrespectful to him or her. If someone is being disruptive, others may leave, thereby refusing to be disrespected.

3. **Decisions made at the meeting apply to everyone whether or not he or she attends.**

In this way individuals soon realize that it is in their best interests to have their opinions heard.

4. **All decisions made at the meeting are in effect until the next regular meeting.**

This rule teaches an important principle: that when we make an agreement with others, it is a form of commitment to those others. If we don't like that agreement, we cannot simply refuse to follow it or change it by ourselves. We are still obligated to live up to our commitment until everyone involved agrees to make a change.

5. **The duration of the meeting depends on the ages of the children.**

For young children, twenty to thirty minutes will probably be the limit. As children grow older and schedules change, each family can decide together what works best for them.

6. **Decisions should be made by consensus.**

By using consensus instead of voting, we develop group solidarity and teach cooperation. When decisions are made by majority rule, factions are likely to develop and competition divides the group. People who don't agree with a rule and feel pressured to follow it may decide that others are unfair and excuse themselves from complying. Many problems arise when family members polarize along the lines of parents versus kids or men versus women. A simple example may suffice:

Karen decided that it would be nice to have a little sister or brother. She brought it up at family meeting. Dad, brother, and Karen voted yes, but Mom voted no. Although the majority liked the idea, it was quite obvious that the veto carried deciding weight.

Consensus encourages cooperation and active participation. It demonstrates that no matter how difficult the problem, if we stay in there long enough, we can come up with a solution that will be acceptable to all. This does not mean that people will always get their first choice, but they may get their second choice, or at least an *acceptable* alternative. If we cannot reach agreement, we put off making a decision until we can come up with a solution that is mutually satisfactory.

7. **Some basic rules for the family meeting should be agreed upon by the group**.

Two simple rules that have proven useful and effective can serve as guidelines for all activities related to the meeting. First, the family meeting is a place where all agree to respect themselves and each other. Second, everyone agrees to help each other. (Since family members may have different ideas about the definition of respect or being helpful, it is useful to develop a "family definition." For example, attack problems, not people; no put-downs; one person speaks at a time; etc.) These rules become the criteria for appropriate behavior and are useful in dealing with some common pitfalls. If a suggestion is given that sounds sarcastic, unfriendly, or insulting, the chairperson may ask, "Do you think that suggestion will be helpful?" or "Do you think that suggestion was respectful to your sister?"

The chairperson can eliminate personal judgment from the response by addressing the person who received the comment, and asking, "Diane, do you think that suggestion will be of help to you?" or, "Diane, did you feel respected by that proposal?" If Diane is asked directly, she gets a chance to say how she perceived the suggestion. The receiver's perception is more important than the observer's perceptions.

8. Parents should make sure they don't talk too much.

Parents sometimes rush in too quickly with solutions and/or easy answers. Holding back gives others an opportunity to formulate and share their ideas.

9. Parents should also avoid rushing in to protect one child or stop disagreement for fear it will end in conflict.

Although the protection might seem to be a good idea, the one being protected might interpret that response as a lack of confidence in her or his ability to solve problems. She or he may even feel insulted by the person who tries to provide protection.

10. Don't seek perfection in the outcome of the meetings.

The purpose of family meetings is to improve family life, to communicate with each other, to celebrate and value each person's uniqueness, to model values, to cooperate, to share responsibility, to teach the importance of helping others, to build self-esteem, to connect with each member, and to discover how fortunate we are to have one another.

How Can Parents Work with Schools?

The second most significant influence on our children's development is their school experience. The classroom is the bridge from the family to the larger society. Teaching only academic subjects is not sufficient; it deprives our children of the opportunity to develop the perceptions and practice the skills necessary to successfully take their place in society. Concerned parents can encourage the schools to establish programs that teach social logic and democratic principles. Since these skills are also necessary for academic success, time spent in their development will be time well spent.

Group discussions and classroom meetings are two of the best ways to teach social competency skills. The format of the classroom meeting can be adapted for many purposes. It can be used to
- Give compliments and appreciations,
- Develop classroom rules together,
- Solve classroom problems,
- Share information,
- Discuss and choose ways to contribute to the school community.

A video training guide for conducting classroom meetings has been developed by Frank Meder and John Platt. It may be purchased through Dynamic Training & Seminars, 8902 Quartzite Circle, Roseville, CA 95661, telephone 800/262-4387.

The Reach Out to Schools: Social Competency Program at Wellesley College's Stone Center uses a format known as the Open Circle to teach students all of the essential skills. The program includes training and support for teachers as well as grade-appropriate lesson plans for conducting open circles twice a week. For more information, contact Reach Out to Schools: Social Competency Program, The Stone Center, Wellesley College, 106 Central Street, Wellesley, MA 02181-8268, telephone 781/283-2847.

References

Bavolek, S. J. (1990). *Shaking, Hitting, Spanking: What to Do Instead.* Park City, Utah: Family Development Resources, Inc.

Bettner, B. L. & Lew, A. (1996). *Raising Kids Who Can.* Newton Centre, Mass.: Connexions Press.

Dreikurs, R. & Soltz, V. (1964). *Children: The Challenge.* New York: Hawthorn Books Inc.

Harrison-Ross, P. & Wyden, B. (1973). *The Black Child: A Parent's Guide.* New York: Peter H. Wyden, Inc.

Appendix I

The Crucial Cs and Rudolf Dreikurs' Short-Range Goals of Misbehavior
Amy Lew and Betty Lou Bettner

Child's belief	Child feels	Child's negative goal	Adult feels	Adult's impulse	Child's response to correction
I only count when I'm being noticed.	insecure alienated	**ATTENTION**	irritated annoyed	**REMIND** What, again?	"temporarily" stops
My strength is in showing you that you can't make me and you can't stop me.	inadequate dependent others are in control	**POWER**	angry challenged	**FIGHT** I insist that you do as I say.	misbehavior intensifies
I knew you were against me. No one really likes me. I'll show you how it feels.	insignificant	**REVENGE** get back get even	hurt or wants to punish	**PUNISH** How could you do this to me? us? them? I'll teach you a lesson.	wants to get even makes self disliked
I can't do anything right so I won't try. If I don't try, my failures won't be so obvious.	inferior useless hopeless	**AVOIDANCE** display of inadequacy	despair I give up. hopeless	**GIVE UP** It's no use.	passive no change more hopeless displays inadequacy

Remember: Misbehavior is a symptom of the child's discouragement about being able to feel the Crucial Cs. Use encouragement and training through natural and logical consequences. Consider and agree on choices together.

Crucial Cs	Constructive Alternatives	Child's belief	Child feels	Child's positive goal
CONNECT	Replace negative attention with positive attention. Plan activities together. Don't ignore the child; ignore the misbehavior. Teach self-sufficiency.	I belong	secure	**COOPER-ATION**
CAPABLE	Don't try to win. Give opportunity and choices so child can display power constructively. Maintain friendly attitude.	I can do it	competent self-control	**SELF-RELIANCE**
COUNT	Avoid anger and hurt feelings. Maintain appreciation in relationship. Offer chances to help. Seek support and help in identifying positives. (Don't give up.)	I matter	significant valuable	**CONTRIBU-TION**
COURAGE	Notice only strengths and ignore the negative. Set up steady exposure to manageable tasks that have a guarantee of success. No criticism.	I can handle what comes	hopeful willing to try	**RESILIENCY**

71

Appendix II

THE CRUCIAL Cs

CONNECT
I need to believe I have a place and I belong.

CAPABLE
I need to believe I can do it.

COUNT
I need to believe I can make a difference.

COURAGE
I need to believe I can handle what comes.

WHEN WE FEEL CONNECTION WE		WHEN WE DON'T FEEL CONNECTION WE	
FEEL	**Secure**	FEEL	**Insecure,** isolated
DO	Reach out	DO	Susceptible to peer pressure
	Make friends		May try to get **attention**
	Cooperate		in negative ways
	NEED	Communication Skills	

WHEN WE FEEL CAPABLE WE		WHEN WE DON'T FEEL CAPABLE WE	
FEEL	**Competent**	FEEL	**Inadequate**
DO	Exhibit self-control	DO	Try to control others and/or become defiant
			May become dependent
	Develop **self-reliance**		Seek **power**
	NEED	Develop self-discipline	

WHEN WE FEEL WE COUNT WE		WHEN WE DON'T FEEL WE COUNT WE	
FEEL	**Valuable**	FEEL	**Insignificant,** hurt
DO	**Contribute**	DO	May try to hurt back or show own pain
			Seek **revenge**
	NEED	Assume responsibility	

WHEN WE HAVE COURAGE WE		WHEN WE DON'T HAVE COURAGE WE	
FEEL	**Equal, confident, hopeful**	FEEL	**Inferior, defeated, hopeless**
DO	Face challenges, willing to try	DO	Give up
	Develop **resiliency**		Use **avoidance**
	NEED	Good Judgment	

Appendix III

Recommended Reading

Albert, Linda. *Cooperative Discipline: How to Manage Your Classroom and Promote Self-Esteem.* Circle Pines, Minn.: American Guidance Service, 1989.

Albert, Linda, and Elizabeth Einstein. *Strengthening Your Stepfamily.* Circle Pines, Minn.: American Guidance Service, 1986.

Bavolek, S. J. *Shaking, Hitting, Spanking: What to Do Instead.* Park City, Utah: Family Development Resources, Inc., 1990.

Bayard, Jean, and Robert Bayard. *How to Deal with Your Acting-Up Teenager,* San Jose, Calif. Accord Press, 1981.

Bettner, Betty Lou, and Amy Lew. *Raising Kids Who Can Series: Parent Study Group Leader's Guide.* Newton Centre, Mass.: Connexions Press, 1998.

Bettner, Betty Lou, and Amy Lew. *Raising Kids Who Can: Use good judgment, Assume responsibility, Communicate effectively, Respect self and others, Cooperate, Develop self-esteem, & Enjoy life.* Newton Centre, Mass.: Connexions Press, 1990, 1996.

Comer, James, and Alvin Poussaint. *Raising Black Children.* New York: Penguin Books. 1992.

Dinkmeyer, Don, and Gary McKay. *Raising a Responsible Child.* New York: Simon and Schuster, 1973.

Dreikurs, Rudolf, and Vicki Soltz. *Children: The Challenge.* New York: Hawthorn Books, Inc., 1964.

Faber, Adele, and Elaine Mazlish. *How to Talk So Your Kids Will Listen and Listen So Your Kids Will Talk.* New York: Avon Books, 1990.

Glenn, H. Stephen, and Jane Nelsen. *Raising Self-Reliant Children In A Self-Indulgent World.* Rocklin, Calif.: Prima Publishing. 1988.

Harrison-Ross, P., & B. Wyden. *The Black Child: A Parent's Guide*. New York: Peter H. Wyden, Inc., 1973.

Lew, Amy, and Betty Lou Bettner. *Responsibility in the Classroom: A Teacher's Guide to Understanding and Motivating Students.* Newton Centre, Mass.: Connexions Press, 1995, 1998.

Lott, Lynn, and Riki Intner. *The Family That Works Together.* Rocklin, Calif.: Prima Publishing, 1994.

Main, Frank, *Perfect Parenting and Other Myths.* Minneapolis, Minn.: CompCare Pub., 1986.

Popkin, Michael. *Active Parenting Today.* Atlanta, Ga.: Active Parenting Publishers, 1993. 1-800-235-7755.

Walton, Francis. *Winning Teenagers Over*. Columbia, So. Car.: Adlerian Child Care Books, 1980.

Weinhaus, Evonne, and Karen Friedman. *Stop Struggling with Your Teen.* St. Louis, Mo.:J.B. Speck Press, 1984.

Appendix IV

About the Authors

Betty Lou Bettner, PhD, CCMHC, is in private practice in individual, couple, and family counseling in Media, Pennsylvania. She is the director of the Family Education Center of the Springfield School District and provides programs for communities and in-service training for educators. Betty Lou is a member and former chair of the Advisory Committee of Children and Youth Services of Delaware County. She was a member of the Delegate Assembly of the North American Society of Adlerian Psychology for ten years and served on the Executive Committee. Betty Lou is on the staff of the International Committee of Adlerian Summer Schools and Institutes.

Amy Lew, PhD, LMHC, LMFT, is a clinical mental health counselor in private practice in couple, individual, and family counseling in Newton, Massachusetts. She serves on the faculty of the Family Institute of Cambridge and the adjunct faculty of the Adler School of Professional Psychology. Amy has served two terms as the vice president of the North American Society of Adlerian Psychology. Amy began her career as an early childhood educator.

In addition to this parent's guide, Amy Lew and Betty Lou Bettner have co-authored a book about family meetings, *Raising Kids Who Can: Use good judgment, Assume responsibility, Communicate effectively, Respect self & others, Cooperate, Develop self-esteem, and Enjoy life*. (The book has been translated into German, Czech, and Estonian.). They have also written a guide for people interested in conducting study groups for parents using the Raising Kids Who Can model, *Raising Kids Who Can Series: A Parent Study Group Leader's Guide*. They have written a companion book for teachers, entitled *Responsibility in the Classroom: A Teacher's Guide to Understanding and Motivating Students*, which covers much of the same material as the parent's guide. Their most recent book, *Cinderella, The Sequel: When The Fairy Tale Ends and Real Life Begins*, uses a lighthearted approach to examine some of the common problems that couples confront and offer suggestions for resolving them.

Appendix V

Other Books by Amy Lew and Betty Lou Bettner

Raising Kids Who Can*:* **Use good judgment, Assume responsibility, Communicate effectively, Respect self & others, Cooperate, Develop self-esteem, and Enjoy life**

"Easy-to-read, logically presented, and filled with many helpful examples. *Raising Kids Who Can* will not only lead to better family meetings, but to better families." —Michael H. Popkin, author of *Active Parenting.*

"This book is a little gem that succeeds in a big way. *Raising Kids Who Can* lays out a readable, doable map for families (and teachers) seeking to develop structure and cooperation in a friendly atmosphere."—*The Family Psychologist*, American Psychological Association.

"Betty Lou Bettner and Amy Lew have created a fresh, insightful synthesis of strategies for becoming a more functional, responsible, and capable family…This is a book about family meetings, but it is also a book about the bigger picture that makes family meetings (and families) work…The book has a practical approach with a clear writing style."—Don Dinkmeyer, Jr., Ph.D., co-author of *The New STEP* (Systematic Training for Effective Parenting), *STEP/Teen,*and *Early Childhood STEP.*

Raising Kids Who Can has been translated into German, Czech, and Estonian.

Responsibility in the Classroom:
A Teacher's Guide to Understanding and Motivating Students

"*In Responsibility in the Classroom* Amy Lew and Betty Lou Bettner present a theoretical construct and practical, accessible strategies and suggestions for developing caring, respectful relationships between teachers and students and among students, and a cooperative classroom community. They provide a framework to help teachers understand children's behavior and develop strategies for achieving the Crucial Cs: feeling connected, capable, knowing that you count, and developing courage. Their approach is an optimistic one…Developing the Crucial Cs becomes a guiding principle in creating a sense of community in the classroom.…"—Pamela Seigle, Director, Reach Out to Schools: Social Competency Program, The Stone Center, Wellesley College.

Raising Kids Who Can Series—Parent Study Group Leader's Guide

This Guide is designed to help parent study group leaders, counselors, social workers, and therapists teach the concepts and strategies outlined in *Raising Kids Who Can* and *A Parent's Guide to Understanding and Motivating Children.*

The Leader's Guide is divided into three sections. The first section provides some tips to help you run your groups. The second and third sections present two courses of six sessions each. Both courses emphasize the importance of developing the Crucial Cs, the beliefs that one is **connected** to others, a part of family and community, **capable** of taking care of oneself; and is valued by others, has the knowledge that one **counts** and makes a difference, and has the **courage** needed to meet life's challenges. The courses also focus on how parents can develop four sets of essential skills in their children: **communication** skills, the ability to use **good judgment** and make wise decisions, **self-discipline,** and the ability to **assume responsibility.**

The design of both courses includes brief presentations of relevant material by the Leader, experiential exercises to reinforce the concepts, time to practice new skills, and the opportunity for parents to get help with their concerns.

CINDERELLA, THE SEQUEL (a fairy tale for adults!)

"When the fairy tale ends and real life begins' is the subtitle of this enchanting and therapeutic tale. Lew and Bettner astutely realize that falling in the love and getting married are only the first 'comparatively easy' steps in the process of building a lasting relationship. In *Cinderella, the Sequel* we see what happened between Cinderella and Prince Charming as they learned to live together and understand one another…Lew and Bettner make very helpful concrete suggestions appropriate for any couple who need help continuing to work on a relationship…This charming metaphor would be invaluable to…couples and individuals who struggle with relationships…"—Terry Kottman, Ph.D. (author of *Adlerian Play Therapy*), *The Family Journal*, International Association of Marriage and Family Counselors.

For information about leader training, in-services, and workshops for parents and teachers, contact Amy Lew and Betty Lou Bettner through Connexions Press.

Ordering Information

Contact Connexions Press at

10 Langley Rd, Suite 200	1 Old State Rd
Newton Centre, MA 02459	Media, PA 19063
tel.: 617/332-3220	tel.: 610/566-1004
fax: 617/332-7863	fax: 610/566-1004
e-mail: connexpr@thecia.net	e-mail: blbettner@aol.com

Books by Amy Lew and Betty Lou Bettner:

A Parent's Guide for Understanding and Motivating Children
ISBN-0-9624841-8-0   Price $8.00

Raising Kids Who Can (1996)
ISBN-0-9624841-7-2   Price: $12.00

Responsibility in the Classroom: A Teacher's Guide to Understanding
and Motivating Students (1998)
ISBN-0-9624841-0-5   Price: $8.00

Raising Kids Who Can Series: Parent Study Group Leader's Guide (1998)
ISBN-0-9624841-1-3   Price: $25.00

Cinderella the Sequel: When the Fairy Tale Ends and Real Life Begins (1996)
ISBN-0-9624841-9-9   Price: $12.00

Shipping and handling:
First book: $3.00   except Leader's Guide: $5.00
Additional books: $1.50   except Leader's Guide: $2.00
5% sales tax in Massachusetts   6% sales tax in Pennsylvania

Quantity discounts available from Connexions Press.

For information about leader training, in-services, and workshops for
parents and teachers, contact Amy Lew and Betty Lou Bettner through
Connexions Press.